A SHROPSHIRE LAD

A
SHROPSHIRE LAD

By
A. E. HOUSMAN

With Wood Engravings by
AGNES MILLER PARKER

GEORGE G. HARRAP & CO. LTD
LONDON TORONTO WELLINGTON SYDNEY

This edition first published in Great Britain 1940
by GEORGE G. HARRAP & CO. LTD
182 High Holborn, London, W.C.1

Reset and reprinted 1953
Reprinted 1954

*Composed in Perpetua type and printed by
Western Printing Services Ltd, Bristol
Made in Great Britain*

CONTENTS

I

1887

From Clee to heaven the beacon burns,
    The shires have seen it plain,
From north and south the sign returns
    And beacons burn again.

Look left, look right, the hills are bright,
    The dales are light between,
Because 'tis fifty years to-night
    That God has saved the Queen.

Now, when the flame they watch not towers
    About the soil they trod,
Lads, we'll remember friends of ours
    Who shared the work with God.

To skies that knit their heartstrings right,
    To fields that bred them brave,
The saviours come not home to-night:
    Themselves they could not save.

It dawns in Asia, tombstones show
    And Shropshire names are read;
And the Nile spills his overflow
    Beside the Severn's dead.

We pledge in peace by farm and town
    The Queen they served in war,
And fire the beacons up and down
    The land they perished for.

"God save the Queen" we living sing,
  From height to height 'tis heard;
And with the rest your voices ring,
  Lads of the Fifty-third.

Oh, God will save her, fear you not:
  Be you the men you've been,
Get you the sons your fathers got,
  And God will save the Queen.

II

LOVELIEST of trees, the cherry now
Is hung with bloom along the bough,
And stands about the woodland ride
Wearing white for Eastertide.

Now, of my threescore years and ten,
Twenty will not come again,
And take from seventy springs a score,
It only leaves me fifty more.

And since to look at things in bloom
Fifty springs are little room,
About the woodlands I will go
To see the cherry hung with snow.

III

THE RECRUIT

Leave your home behind, lad,
   And reach your friends your hand,
And go, and luck go with you
   While Ludlow tower shall stand.

Oh, come you home of Sunday
   When Ludlow streets are still
And Ludlow bells are calling
   To farm and lane and mill,

Or come you home on Monday
   When Ludlow market hums
And Ludlow chimes are playing
   "The conquering hero comes,"

Come you home a hero,
   Or come not home at all,
The lads you leave will mind you
   Till Ludlow tower shall fall.

And you will list the bugle
   That blows in lands of morn,
And make the foes of England
   Be sorry you were born.

And you till trump of doomsday
   On lands of morn may lie,
And make the hearts of comrades
   Be heavy where you die.

Leave your home behind you,
  Your friends by field and town:
Oh, town and field will mind you
  Till Ludlow tower is down.

IV

REVEILLE

WAKE: the silver dusk returning
    Up the beach of darkness brims,
And the ship of sunrise burning
    Strands upon the eastern rims.

Wake: the vaulted shadow shatters,
    Trampled to the floor it spanned,
And the tent of night in tatters
    Straws the sky-pavilioned land.

Up, lad, up, 'tis late for lying:
    Hear the drums of morning play;
Hark, the empty highways crying
    " Who'll beyond the hills away? "

Towns and countries woo together,
    Forelands beacon, belfries call;
Never lad that trod on leather
    Lived to feast his heart with all.

Up, lad: thews that lie and cumber
    Sunlit pallets never thrive;
Morns abed and daylight slumber
    Were not meant for man alive.

Clay lies still, but blood's a rover;
    Breath's a ware that will not keep.
Up, lad: when the journey's over
    There'll be time enough to sleep.

V

Oн see how thick the goldcup flowers
    Are lying in field and lane,
With dandelions to tell the hours
    That never are told again.
Oh may I squire you round the meads
    And pick you posies gay?
—'Twill do no harm to take my arm.
    " You may, young man, you may."

Ah, spring was sent for lass and lad,
    'Tis now the blood runs gold,
And man and maid had best be glad
    Before the world is old.
What flowers to-day may flower to-morrow,
    But never as good as new.
—Suppose I wound my arm right round—
    " 'Tis true, young man, 'tis true."

Some lads there are, 'tis shame to say,
    That only court to thieve,
And once they bear the bloom away
    'Tis little enough they leave.
Then keep your heart for men like me
    And safe from trustless chaps.
My love is true and all for you.
    " Perhaps, young man, perhaps."

Oh, look in my eyes, then, can you doubt?
   —Why, 'tis a mile from town.
How green the grass is all about!
   We might as well sit down.
—Ah, life, what is it but a flower?
   Why must true lovers sigh?
Be kind, have pity, my own, my pretty,—
   " Good-bye, young man, good-bye."

VI

W<small>HEN</small> the lad for longing sighs,
  Mute and dull of cheer and pale,
If at death's own door he lies,
  Maiden, you can heal his ail.

Lovers' ills are all to buy:
  The wan look, the hollow tone,
The hung head, the sunken eye,
  You can have them for your own.

Buy them, buy them: eve and morn
  Lovers' ills are all to sell.
Then you can lie down forlorn;
  But the lover will be well.

VII

When smoke stood up from Ludlow,
  And mist blew off from Teme,
And blithe afield to ploughing
  Against the morning beam
  I strode beside my team,

The blackbird in the coppice
  Looked out to see me stride,
And hearkened as I whistled
  The trampling team beside,
  And fluted and replied:

" Lie down, lie down, young yeoman;
  What use to rise and rise?
Rise man a thousand mornings
  Yet down at last he lies,
  And then the man is wise."

I heard the tune he sang me,
  And spied his yellow bill;
I picked a stone and aimed it
  And threw it with a will:
  Then the bird was still.

Then my soul within me
  Took up the blackbird's strain,
And still beside the horses
  Along the dewy lane
  It sang the song again:

" Lie down, lie down, young yeoman;
    The sun moves always west;
The road one treads to labour
    Will lead one home to rest,
    And that will be the best."

VIII

" Farewell to barn and stack and tree,
  Farewell to Severn shore.
Terence, look your last at me,
  For I come home no more.

" The sun burns on the half-mown hill,
  By now the blood is dried;
And Maurice amongst the hay lies still
  And my knife is in his side.

" My mother thinks us long away;
  'Tis time the field were mown.
She had two sons at rising day,
  To-night she'll be alone.

" And here's a bloody hand to shake,
  And oh, man, here's good-bye;
We'll sweat no more on scythe and rake,
  My bloody hands and I.

" I wish you strength to bring you pride,
  And a love to keep you clean,
And I wish you luck, come Lammastide,
  At racing on the green.

" Long for me the rick will wait,
  And long will wait the fold,
And long will stand the empty plate,
  And dinner will be cold."

IX

On moonlit heath and lonesome bank
  The sheep beside me graze;
And yon the gallows used to clank
  Fast by the four cross ways.

A careless shepherd once would keep
  The flocks by moonlight there,[1]
And high amongst the glimmering sheep
  The dead man stood on air.

They hang us now in Shrewsbury jail:
  The whistles blow forlorn,
And trains all night groan on the rail
  To men that die at morn.

There sleeps in Shrewsbury jail to-night,
  Or wakes, as may betide,
A better lad, if things went right,
  Than most that sleep outside.

And naked to the hangman's noose
  The morning clocks will ring
A neck God made for other use
  Than strangling in a string.

And sharp the link of life will snap,
  And dead on air will stand
Heels that held up as straight a chap
  As treads upon the land.

[1] Hanging in chains was called keeping sheep by moonlight.

So here I'll watch the night and wait
    To see the morning shine,
When he will hear the stroke of eight
    And not the stroke of nine;

And wish my friend as sound a sleep
    As lads' I did not know,
That shepherded the moonlit sheep
    A hundred years ago.

MARCH

THE Sun at noon to higher air,
Unharnessing the silver Pair
That late before his chariot swam,
Rides on the gold wool of the Ram.

So braver notes the storm-cock sings
To start the rusted wheel of things,
And brutes in field and brutes in pen
Leap that the world goes round again.

The boys are up the woods with day
To fetch the daffodils away,
And home at noonday from the hills
They bring no dearth of daffodils.

Afield for palms the girls repair,
And sure enough the palms are there,
And each will find by hedge or pond
Her waving silver-tufted wand.

In farm and field through all the shire
The eye beholds the heart's desire;
Ah, let not only mine be vain,
For lovers should be loved again.

On your midnight pallet lying,
　Listen, and undo the door:
Lads that waste the night in sighing
　In the dark should sigh no more;
Night should ease a lover's sorrow;
Therefore, since I go to-morrow,
　Pity me before.

In the land to which I travel,
　The far dwelling, let me say—
Once, if here the couch is gravel,
　In a kinder bed I lay,
And the breast the darnel smothers
Rested once upon another's
　When it was not clay.

XII

WHEN I watch the living meet,
　　And the moving pageant file
Warm and breathing through the street
　　Where I lodge a little while,

If the heats of hate and lust
　　In the house of flesh are strong,
Let me mind the house of dust
　　Where my sojourn shall be long.

In the nation that is not
　　Nothing stands that stood before;
There revenges are forgot,
　　And the hater hates no more;

Lovers lying two and two
　　Ask not whom they sleep beside,
And the bridegroom all night through
　　Never turns him to the bride.

XIII

When I was one-and-twenty
  I heard a wise man say,
" Give crowns and pounds and guineas
  But not your heart away;
Give pearls away and rubies
  But keep your fancy free."
But I was one-and-twenty,
  No use to talk to me.

When I was one-and-twenty
  I heard him say again,
" The heart out of the bosom
  Was never given in vain;
'Tis paid with sighs a plenty
  And sold for endless rue."
And I am two-and-twenty,
  And oh, 'tis true, 'tis true.

XIV

THERE pass the careless people
    That call their souls their own:
Here by the road I loiter,
    How idle and alone.

Ah, past the plunge of plummet,
    In seas I cannot sound,
My heart and soul and senses,
    World without end, are drowned.

His folly has not fellow
    Beneath the blue of day
That gives to man or woman
    His heart and soul away.

There flowers no balm to sain him
    From east of earth to west
That's lost for everlasting
    The heart out of his breast.

Here by the labouring highway
    With empty hands I stroll:
Sea-deep, till doomsday morning,
    Lie lost my heart and soul.

XV

Look not in my eyes, for fear
  They mirror true the sight I see,
And there you find your face too clear
  And love it and be lost like me.
One the long nights through must lie
  Spent in star-defeated sighs,
But why should you as well as I
  Perish? gaze not in my eyes.

A Grecian lad, as I hear tell,
  One that many loved in vain,
Looked into a forest well
  And never looked away again.
There, when the turf in springtime flowers,
  With downward eye and gazes sad,
Stands amid the glancing showers
  A jonquil, not a Grecian lad.

XVI

It nods and curtseys and recovers
　　When the wind blows above,
The nettle on the graves of lovers
　　That hanged themselves for love.

The nettle nods, the wind blows over,
　　The man, he does not move,
The lover of the grave, the lover
　　That hanged himself for love.

XVII

Twice a week the winter thorough
  Here stood I to keep the goal:
Football then was fighting sorrow
  For the young man's soul.

Now in Maytime to the wicket
  Out I march with bat and pad:
See the son of grief at cricket
  Trying to be glad.

Try I will; no harm in trying:
  Wonder 'tis how little mirth
Keeps the bones of man from lying
  On the bed of earth.

XVIII

Oʜ, when I was in love with you,
  Then I was clean and brave,
And miles around the wonder grew
  How well did I behave.

And now the fancy passes by,
  And nothing will remain,
And miles around they'll say that I
  Am quite myself again.

XIX

TO AN ATHLETE DYING YOUNG

THE time you won your town the race
We chaired you through the market-place;
Man and boy stood cheering by,
And home we brought you shoulder-high.

To-day, the road all runners come,
Shoulder-high we bring you home,
And set you at your threshold down,
Townsman of a stiller town.

Smart lad, to slip betimes away
From fields where glory does not stay
And early though the laurel grows
It withers quicker than the rose.

Eyes the shady night has shut
Cannot see the record cut,
And silence sounds no worse than cheers
After earth has stopped the ears:

Now you will not swell the rout
Of lads that wore their honours out,
Runners whom renown outran
And the name died before the man.

So set, before its echoes fade,
The fleet foot on the sill of shade,
And hold to the low lintel up
The still-defended challenge-cup.

And round that early-laurelled head
Will flock to gaze the strengthless dead,
And find unwithered on its curls
The garland briefer than a girl's.

XX

Oʜ fair enough are sky and plain,
  But I know fairer far:
Those are as beautiful again
  That in the water are;

The pools and rivers wash so clean
  The trees and clouds and air,
The like on earth was never seen,
  And oh that I were there.

These are the thoughts I often think
  As I stand gazing down
In act upon the cressy brink
  To strip and dive and drown;

But in the golden-sanded brooks
  And azure meres I spy
A silly lad that longs and looks
  And wishes he were I.

XXI

BREDON[1] HILL

In summertime on Bredon
  The bells they sound so clear;
Round both the shires they ring them
  In steeples far and near,
  A happy noise to hear.

Here of a Sunday morning
  My love and I would lie,
And see the coloured counties,
  And hear the larks so high
  About us in the sky.

The bells would ring to call her
  In valleys miles away:
" Come all to church, good people;
  Good people, come and pray."
  But here my love would stay.

And I would turn and answer
  Among the springing thyme,
" Oh, peal upon our wedding,
  And we will hear the chime,
  And come to church in time."

[1] Pronounced Breedon.

But when the snows at Christmas
    On Bredon top were strown,
My love rose up so early
    And stole out unbeknown
    And went to church alone.

They tolled the one bell only,
    Groom there was none to see,
The mourners followed after,
    And so to church went she,
    And would not wait for me.

The bells they sound on Bredon,
    And still the steeples hum.
" Come all to church, good people,"—
    Oh, noisy bells, be dumb;
    I hear you, I will come.

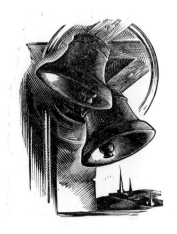

XXII

THE street sounds to the soldiers' tread,
   And out we troop to see:
A single redcoat turns his head,
   He turns and looks at me.

My man, from sky to sky's so far,
   We never crossed before;
Such leagues apart the world's ends are,
   We're like to meet no more;

What thoughts at heart have you and I
   We cannot stop to tell;
But dead or living, drunk or dry,
   Soldier, I wish you well.

XXIII

The lads in their hundreds to Ludlow
                  come in for the fair,
There's men from the barn and the forge
                  and the mill and the fold,
The lads for the girls and the lads
                  for the liquor are there,
And there with the rest are the lads
                  that will never be old.

There's chaps from the town and the field
                  and the till and the cart,
And many to count are the stalwart,
                  and many the brave,
And many the handsome of face
                  and the handsome of heart,
And few that will carry their looks
                  or their truth to the grave.

I wish one could know them,
                  I wish there were tokens to tell
The fortunate fellows that now
                  you can never discern;
And then one could talk with them friendly
                  and wish them farewell
And watch them depart on the way
                  that they will not return.

But now you may stare as you like
        and there's nothing to scan;
And brushing your elbow unguessed-at
            and not to be told
They carry back bright to the coiner
            the mintage of man,
The lads that will die in their glory
            and never be old.

XXIV

Say, lad, have you things to do?
  Quick then, while your day's at prime.
Quick, and if 'tis work for two,
  Here am I, man: now's your time.

Send me now, and I shall go;
  Call me, I shall hear you call;
Use me ere they lay me low
  Where a man's no use at all;

Ere the wholesome flesh decay,
  And the willing nerve be numb,
And the lips lack breath to say,
  " No, my lad, I cannot come."

XXV

This time of year a twelvemonth past,
    When Fred and I would meet,
We needs must jangle, till at last
    We fought and I was beat.

So then the summer fields about,
    Till rainy days began,
Rose Harland on her Sundays out
    Walked with the better man.

The better man she walks with still,
    Though now 'tis not with Fred:
A lad that lives and has his will
    Is worth a dozen dead.

Fred keeps the house all kinds of weather,
    And clay's the house he keeps;
When Rose and I walk out together
    Stock-still lies Fred and sleeps.

XXVI

ALONG the field as we came by
A year ago, my love and I,
The aspen over stile and stone
Was talking to itself alone.
" Oh who are these that kiss and pass?
A country lover and his lass;
Two lovers looking to be wed;
And time shall put them both to bed,
But she shall lie with earth above,
And he beside another love."

And sure enough beneath the tree
There walks another love with me,
And overhead the aspen heaves
Its rainy-sounding silver leaves;
And I spell nothing in their stir,
But now perhaps they speak to her,
And plain for her to understand
They talk about a time at hand
When I shall sleep with clover clad,
And she beside another lad.

XXVII

"Is my team ploughing,
  That I was used to drive
And hear the harness jingle
  When I was man alive?"

Ay, the horses trample,
  The harness jingles now;
No change though you lie under
  The land you used to plough.

"Is football playing
  Along the river shore,
With lads to chase the leather,
  Now I stand up no more?"

Ay, the ball is flying,
  The lads play heart and soul;
The goal stands up, the keeper
  Stands up to keep the goal.

"Is my girl happy,
  That I thought hard to leave,
And has she tired of weeping
  As she lies down at eve?"

Ay, she lies down lightly,
  She lies not down to weep:
Your girl is well contented.
  Be still, my lad, and sleep.

" Is my friend hearty,
    Now I am thin and pine,
And has he found to sleep in
    A better bed than mine ? "

Yes, lad, I lie easy,
    I lie as lads would choose;
I cheer a dead man's sweetheart,
    Never ask me whose.

XXVIII

THE WELSH MARCHES

HIGH the vanes of Shrewsbury gleam
Islanded in Severn stream;
The bridges from the steepled crest
Cross the water east and west.

The flag of morn in conqueror's state
Enters at the English gate:
The vanquished eve, as night prevails,
Bleeds upon the road to Wales.

Ages since the vanquished bled
Round my mother's marriage-bed;
There the ravens feasted far
About the open house of war:

When Severn down to Buildwas ran
Coloured with the death of man,
Couched upon her brother's grave
The Saxon got me on the slave.

The sound of fight is silent long
That began the ancient wrong;
Long the voice of tears is still
That wept of old the endless ill.

In my heart it has not died,
The war that sleeps on Severn side;
They cease not fighting, east and west,
On the marches of my breast.

Here the truceless armies yet
Trample, rolled in blood and sweat;
They kill and kill and never die;
And I think that each is I.

None will part us, none undo
The knot that makes one flesh of two,
Sick with hatred, sick with pain,
Strangling—When shall we be slain?

When shall I be dead and rid
Of the wrong my father did?
How long, how long, till spade and hearse
Put to sleep my mother's curse?

THE LENT LILY

'Tis spring; come out to ramble
  The hilly brakes around,
For under thorn and bramble
  About the hollow ground
  The primroses are found.

And there's the windflower chilly
  With all the winds at play,
And there's the Lenten lily
  That has not long to stay
  And dies on Easter day.

And since till girls go maying
  You find the primrose still,
And find the windflower playing
  With every wind at will,
  But not the daffodil,

Bring baskets now, and sally
  Upon the spring's array,
And bear from hill and valley
  The daffodil away
  That dies on Easter day.

OTHERS, I am not the first,
Have willed more mischief than they durst:
If in the breathless night I too
Shiver now, 'tis nothing new.

More than I, if truth were told,
Have stood and sweated hot and cold,
And through their reins in ice and fire
Fear contended with desire.

Agued once like me were they,
But I like them shall win my way
Lastly to the bed of mould
Where there's neither heat nor cold.

But from my grave across my brow
Plays no wind of healing now,
And fire and ice within me fight
Beneath the suffocating night.

XXXI

On Wenlock Edge the wood's in trouble;
  His forest fleece the Wrekin heaves;
The gale, it plies the saplings double,
  And thick on Severn snow the leaves.

'Twould blow like this through
                        holt and hanger
  When Uricon the city stood:
'Tis the old wind in the old anger,
  But then it threshed another wood.

Then, 'twas before my time, the Roman
  At yonder heaving hill would stare:
The blood that warms an English yeoman,
  The thoughts that hurt him,
                      they were there.

There, like the wind through woods in riot,
  Through him the gale of life blew high;
The tree of man was never quiet:
  Then 'twas the Roman, now 'tis I.

The gale, it plies the saplings double,
  It blows so hard, 'twill soon be gone:
To-day the Roman and his trouble
  Are ashes under Uricon.

XXXII

From far, from eve and morning
  And yon twelve-winded sky,
The stuff of life to knit me
  Blew hither: here am I.

Now—for a breath I tarry
  Nor yet disperse apart—
Take my hand quick and tell me,
  What have you in your heart.

Speak now, and I will answer;
  How shall I help you, say;
Ere to the wind's twelve quarters
  I take my endless way.

XXXIII

If truth in hearts that perish
    Could move the powers on high,
I think the love I bear you
    Should make you not to die.

Sure, sure, if stedfast meaning,
    If single thought could save,
The world might end to-morrow,
    You should not see the grave.

This long and sure-set liking,
    This boundless will to please,
—Oh, you should live for ever
    If there were help in these.

But now, since all is idle,
    To this lost heart be kind,
Ere to a town you journey
    Where friends are ill to find.

XXXIV

THE NEW MISTRESS

"Oh, *sick I am to see you,*
            will you never let me be?
You may be good for something,
            but you are not good for me.
Oh, go where you are wanted,
            for you are not wanted here."
And that was all the farewell
            when I parted from my dear.

" I will go where I am wanted,
            to a lady born and bred
Who will dress me free for nothing
            in a uniform of red;
She will not be sick to see me
            if I only keep it clean:
I will go where I am wanted
            for a soldier of the Queen.

" I will go where I am wanted,
            for the sergeant does not mind;
He may be sick to see me
            but he treats me very kind:
He gives me beer and breakfast
            and a ribbon for my cap,
And I never knew a sweetheart
            spend her money on a chap.

" I will go where I am wanted,
        where there's room for one or two,
And the men are none too many
        for the work there is to do;
Where the standing line wears thinner
        and the dropping dead lie thick;
And the enemies of England
        they shall see me and be sick."

XXXV

On the idle hill of summer,
　Sleepy with the flow of streams,
Far I hear the steady drummer
　Drumming like a noise in dreams.

Far and near and low and louder
　On the roads of earth go by,
Dear to friends and food for powder,
　Soldiers marching, all to die.

East and west on fields forgotten
　Bleach the bones of comrades slain,
Lovely lads and dead and rotten;
　None that go return again.

Far the calling bugles hollo,
　High the screaming fife replies,
Gay the files of scarlet follow:
　Woman bore me, I will rise.

XXXVI

Wʜɪᴛᴇ in the moon the long road lies,
  The moon stands blank above;
White in the moon the long road lies
  That leads me from my love.

Still hangs the hedge without a gust,
  Still, still the shadows stay:
My feet upon the moonlit dust
  Pursue the ceaseless way.

The world is round, so travellers tell,
  And straight though reach the track,
Trudge on, trudge on, 'twill all be well,
  The way will guide one back.

But ere the circle homeward hies
  Far, far, must it remove:
White in the moon the long road lies
  That leads me from my love.

XXXVII

As through the wild green hills of Wyre
The train ran, changing sky and shire,
And far behind, a fading crest,
Low in the forsaken west
Sank the high-reared head of Clee,
My hand lay empty on my knee.
Aching on my knee it lay:
That morning half a shire away
So many an honest fellow's fist
Had well-nigh wrung it from the wrist.
Hand, said I, since now we part
From fields and men we know by heart,
For strangers' faces, strangers' lands,—
Hand, you have held true fellows' hands.
Be clean then; rot before you do
A thing they'd not believe of you.
You and I must keep from shame
In London streets the Shropshire name;
On banks of Thames they must not say
Severn breeds worse men than they;
And friends abroad must bear in mind
Friends at home they leave behind.
Oh, I shall be stiff and cold
When I forget you, hearts of gold;
The land where I shall mind you not
Is the land where all's forgot.
And if my foot returns no more
To Teme nor Corve nor Severn shore,
Luck, my lads, be with you still

By falling stream and standing hill,
By climbing tower and whispering tree,
Men that made a man of me.
About your work in town and farm
Still you'll keep my head from harm,
Still you'll help me, hands that gave
A grasp to friend me to the grave.

XXXVIII

THE winds out of the west land blow,
  My friends have breathed them there;
Warm with the blood of lads I know
  Comes east the sighing air.

It fanned their temples, filled their lungs,
  Scattered their forelocks free;
My friends made words of it with tongues
  That talk no more to me.

Their voices, dying as they fly,
  Loose on the wind are sown;
The names of men blow soundless by,
  My fellows' and my own.

Oh lads, at home I heard you plain,
  But here your speech is still,
And down the sighing wind in vain
  You hollo from the hill.

The wind and I, we both were there,
  But neither long abode;
Now through the friendless world we fare
  And sigh upon the road.

XXXIX

'Tis time, I think, by Wenlock town
  The golden broom should blow;
The hawthorn sprinkled up and down
  Should charge the land with snow.

Spring will not wait the loiterer's time
  Who keeps so long away;
So others wear the broom and climb
  The hedgerows heaped with may.

Oh tarnish late on Wenlock Edge,
  Gold that I never see;
Lie long, high snowdrifts in the hedge
  That will not shower on me.

Into my heart an air that kills
  From yon far country blows:
What are those blue remembered hills,
  What spires, what farms are those?

That is the land of lost content,
  I see it shining plain,
The happy highways where I went
  And cannot come again.

XLI

In my own shire, if I was sad,
Homely comforters I had:
The earth, because my heart was sore,
Sorrowed for the son she bore;
And standing hills, long to remain,
Shared their short-lived comrade's pain.
And bound for the same bourn as I,
On every road I wandered by,
Trod beside me, close and dear,
The beautiful and death-struck year:
Whether in the woodland brown
I heard the beechnut rustle down,
And saw the purple crocus pale
Flower about the autumn dale;
Or littering far the fields of May
Lady-smocks a-bleaching lay,
And like a skylit water stood
The bluebells in the azured wood.

Yonder, lightening other loads,
The seasons range the country roads,
But here in London streets I ken
No such helpmates, only men;
And these are not in plight to bear,
If they would, another's care.
They have enough as 'tis: I see
In many an eye that measures me
The mortal sickness of a mind
Too unhappy to be kind.

Undone with misery, all they can
Is to hate their fellow man;
And till they drop they needs must still
Look at you and wish you ill.

XLII

THE MERRY GUIDE

O<small>NCE</small> in the wind of morning
   I ranged the thymy wold;
The world-wide air was azure
   And all the brooks ran gold.

There through the dews beside me
   Behold a youth that trod,
With feathered cap on forehead,
   And poised a golden rod.

With mien to match the morning
   And gay delightful guise
And friendly brows and laughter
   He looked me in the eyes.

Oh whence, I asked, and whither?
   He smiled and would not say,
And looked at me and beckoned
   And laughed and led the way.

And with kind looks and laughter
   And nought to say beside
We two went on together,
   I and my happy guide.

Across the glittering pastures
   And empty upland still
And solitude of shepherds
   High in the folded hill,

By hanging woods and hamlets
   That gaze through orchards down
On many a windmill turning
   And far-discovered town,

With gay regards of promise
   And sure unslackened stride
And smiles and nothing spoken
   Led on my merry guide.

By blowing realms of woodland
   With sunstruck vanes afield
And cloud-led shadows sailing
   About the windy weald,

By valley-guarded granges
   And silver waters wide,
Content at heart I followed
   With my delightful guide.

And like the cloudy shadows
   Across the country blown
We two fare on for ever,
   But not we two alone.

With the great gale we journey
   That breathes from gardens thinned,
Borne in the drift of blossoms
   Whose petals throng the wind;

Buoyed on the heaven-heard whisper
  Of dancing leaflets whirled
From all the woods that autumn
  Bereaves in all the world.

And midst the fluttering legion
  Of all that ever died
I follow, and before us
  Goes the delightful guide,

With lips that brim with laughter
  But never once respond,
And feet that fly on feathers,
  And serpent-circled wand.

THE IMMORTAL PART

W<small>HEN</small> I meet the morning beam,
Or lay me down at night to dream,
I hear my bones within me say,
" Another night, another day.

" When shall this slough of sense be cast,
This dust of thought be laid at last,
The man of flesh and soul be slain
And the man of bone remain?

" This tongue that talks, these
                  lungs that shout,
These thews that hustle us about,
This brain that fills the skull with schemes,
And its humming hive of dreams,—

" These to-day are proud in power
And lord it in their little hour:
The immortal bones obey control
Of dying flesh and dying soul.

" 'Tis long till eve and morn are gone:
Slow the endless night comes on,
And late to fulness grows the birth
That shall last as long as earth.

" Wanderers eastward, wanderers west,
Know you why you cannot rest?
'Tis that every mother's son
Travails with a skeleton.

" Lie down in the bed of dust;
Bear the fruit that bear you must;
Bring the eternal seed to light,
And morn is all the same as night.

" Rest you so from trouble sore,
Fear the heat o' the sun no more,
Nor the snowing winter wild,
Now you labour not with child.

" Empty vessel, garment cast,
We that wore you long shall last.
—Another night, another day."
So my bones within me say.

Therefore they shall do my will
To-day while I am master still,
And flesh and soul, now both are strong,
Shall hale the sullen slaves along,

Before this fire of sense decay,
This smoke of thought blow clean away,
And leave with ancient night alone
The stedfast and enduring bone.

XLIV

Shot? so quick, so clean an ending?
  Oh that was right, lad, that was brave:
Yours was not an ill for mending,
  'Twas best to take it to the grave.

Oh you had forethought, you could reason,
  And saw your road and where it led,
And early wise and brave in season
  Put the pistol to your head.

Oh soon, and better so than later
  After long disgrace and scorn,
You shot dead the household traitor,
  The soul that should not have been born.

Right you guessed the rising morrow
  And scorned to tread the mire you must:
Dust's your wages, son of sorrow,
  But men may come to worse than dust.

Souls undone, undoing others,—
  Long time since the tale began.
You would not live to wrong your brothers:
  Oh lad, you died as fits a man.

Now to your grave shall friend and stranger
  With ruth and some with envy come:
Undishonoured, clear of danger,
  Clean of guilt, pass hence and home.

Turn safe to rest, no dreams, no waking;
  And here, man, here's the wreath I've made:
'Tis not a gift that's worth the taking,
  But wear it and it will not fade.

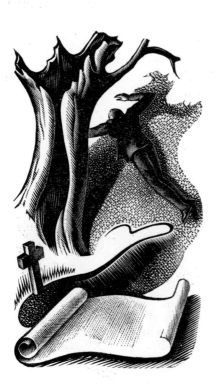

I_F it chance your eye offend you,
  Pluck it out, lad, and be sound:
'Twill hurt, but here are salves to friend you,
  And many a balsam grows on ground.

And if your hand or foot offend you,
  Cut it off, lad, and be whole;
But play the man, stand up and end you,
  When your sickness is your soul.

XLVI

BRING, in this timeless grave to throw,
No cypress, sombre on the snow;
Snap not from the bitter yew
His leaves that live December through;
Break no rosemary, bright with rime
And sparkling to the cruel clime;
Nor plod the winter land to look
For willows in the icy brook
To cast them leafless round him: bring
No spray that ever buds in spring.

But if the Christmas field has kept
Awns the last gleaner overstept,
Or shrivelled flax, whose flower is blue
A single season, never two;
Or if one haulm whose year is o'er
Shivers on the upland frore,
—Oh, bring from hill and stream and plain
Whatever will not flower again,
To give him comfort: he and those
Shall bide eternal bedfellows
Where low upon the couch he lies
Whence he never shall arise.

THE CARPENTER'S SON

" Here the hangman stops his cart:
Now the best of friends must part.
Fare you well, for ill fare I:
Live, lads, and I will die.

" Oh, at home had I but stayed
'Prenticed to my father's trade,
Had I stuck to plane and adze,
I had not been lost, my lads.

" Then I might have built perhaps
Gallows-trees for other chaps,
Never dangled on my own,
Had I but left ill alone.

" Now, you see, they hang me high,
And the people passing by
Stop to shake their fists and curse;
So 'tis come from ill to worse.

" Here hang I, and right and left
Two poor fellows hang for theft:
All the same's the luck we prove,
Though the midmost hangs for love.

" Comrades all, that stand and gaze,
Walk henceforth in other ways;
See my neck and save your own:
Comrades all, leave ill alone.

72

" Make some day a decent end,
Shrewder fellows than your friend.
Fare you well, for ill fare I:
Live, lads, and I will die."

XLVIII

Be still, my soul, be still;
              the arms you bear are brittle,
    Earth and high heaven are fixt
              of old and founded strong.
Think rather,—call to thought,
              if now you grieve a little,
    The days when we had rest,
              O soul, for they were long.

Men loved unkindness then,
              but lightless in the quarry
    I slept and saw not; tears fell down,
              I did not mourn;
Sweat ran and blood sprang out
              and I was never sorry:
    Then it was well with me,
              in days ere I was born.

Now, and I muse for why
              and never find the reason,
    I pace the earth, and drink the air,
              and feel the sun.
Be still, be still, my soul;
              it is but for a season:
    Let us endure an hour
              and see injustice done.

Ay, look: high heaven and earth
                    ail from the prime foundation;
All thoughts to rive the heart are here,
                    and all are vain:
Horror and scorn and hate
                    and fear and indignation—
Oh why did I awake?
                    when shall I sleep again?

Think no more, lad; laugh, be jolly:
  Why should men make haste to die?
Empty heads and tongues a-talking
Make the rough road easy walking,
And the feather pate of folly
  Bears the falling sky.

Oh, 'tis jesting, dancing, drinking
  Spins the heavy world around.
If young hearts were not so clever,
Oh, they would be young for ever:
Think no more; 'tis only thinking
  Lays lads underground.

L

Clunton and Clunbury,
Clungunford and Clun,
Are the quietest places
Under the sun.

In valleys of springs of rivers,
    By Ony and Teme and Clun,
The country for easy livers,
    The quietest under the sun,

We still had sorrows to lighten,
    One could not be always glad,
And lads knew trouble at Knighton
    When I was a Knighton lad.

By bridges that Thames runs under,
    In London, the town built ill,
'Tis sure small matter for wonder
    If sorrow is with one still.

And if as a lad grows older
    The troubles he bears are more,
He carries his griefs on a shoulder
    That handselled them long before.

Where shall one halt to deliver
    This luggage I'd lief set down?
Not Thames, not Teme is the river,
    Nor London nor Knighton the town:

'Tis a long way further than Knighton,
  A quieter place than Clun,
Where doomsday may thunder and lighten
  And little 'twill matter to one.

Loitering with a vacant eye
Along the Grecian gallery,
And brooding on my heavy ill,
I met a statue standing still.
Still in marble stone stood he,
And stedfastly he looked at me.
" Well met," I thought the look would say,
" We both were fashioned far away;
We neither knew, when we were young,
These Londoners we live among."

Still he stood and eyed me hard,
An earnest and a grave regard:
" What, lad, drooping with your lot?
I too would be where I am not.
I too survey that endless line
Of men whose thoughts are not as mine.
Years, ere you stood up from rest,
On my neck the collar prest;
Years, when you lay down your ill,
I shall stand and bear it still.
Courage, lad, 'tis not for long:
Stand, quit you like stone, be strong."
So I thought his look would say;
And light on me my trouble lay,
And I stept out in flesh and bone
Manful like the man of stone.

LII

FAR in a western brookland
  That bred me long ago
The poplars stand and tremble
  By pools I used to know.

There, in the windless night-time,
  The wanderer, marvelling why,
Halts on the bridge to hearken
  How soft the poplars sigh.

He hears: no more remembered
  In fields where I was known,
Here I lie down in London
  And turn to rest alone.

There, by the starlit fences,
  The wanderer halts and hears
My soul that lingers sighing
  About the glimmering weirs.

LIII

THE TRUE LOVER

THE lad came to the door at night,
  When lovers crown their vows,
And whistled soft and out of sight
  In shadow of the boughs.

" I shall not vex you with my face
  Henceforth, my love, for aye;
So take me in your arms a space
  Before the east is grey.

" When I from hence away am past
  I shall not find a bride,
And you shall be the first and last
  I ever lay beside."

She heard and went and knew not why;
  Her heart to his she laid;
Light was the air beneath the sky
  But dark under the shade.

" Oh do you breathe, lad, that your breast
  Seems not to rise and fall,
And here upon my bosom prest
  There beats no heart at all?"

" Oh loud, my girl, it once would knock,
  You should have felt it then;
But since for you I stopped the clock
  It never goes again."

"Oh lad, what is it, lad, that drips
　　Wet from your neck on mine?
What is it falling on my lips,
　　My lad, that tastes of brine?"

"Oh like enough 'tis blood, my dear,
　　For when the knife has slit
The throat across from ear to ear
　　'Twill bleed because of it."

Under the stars the air was light
　　But dark below the boughs,
The still air of the speechless night,
　　When lovers crown their vows.

Wɪᴛʜ rue my heart is laden
   For golden friends I had,
For many a rose-lipt maiden
   And many a lightfoot lad.

By brooks too broad for leaping
   The lightfoot boys are laid;
The rose-lipt girls are sleeping
   In fields where roses fade.

LV

Westward on the high-hilled plains
    Where for me the world began,
Still, I think, in newer veins
    Frets the changeless blood of man.

Now that other lads than I
    Strip to bathe on Severn shore,
They, no help, for all they try,
    Tread the mill I trod before.

There, when hueless is the west
    And the darkness hushes wide,
Where the lad lies down to rest
    Stands the troubled dream beside.

There, on thoughts that once were mine,
    Day looks down the eastern steep,
And the youth at morning shine
    Makes the vow he will not keep.

THE DAY OF BATTLE

" Far I hear the bugle blow
To call me where I would not go,
And the guns begin the song,
' Soldier, fly or stay for long.'

" Comrade, if to turn and fly
Made a soldier never die,
Fly I would, for who would not?
'Tis sure no pleasure to be shot.

" But since the man that runs away
Lives to die another day,
And cowards' funerals, when they come,
Are not wept so well at home,

" Therefore, though the best is bad,
Stand and do the best, my lad;
Stand and fight and see your slain,
And take the bullet in your brain."

LVII

You smile upon your friend to-day,
  To-day his ills are over;
You hearken to the lover's say,
  And happy is the lover.

'Tis late to hearken, late to smile,
  But better late than never:
I shall have lived a little while
  Before I die for ever.

LVIII

W HEN I came last to Ludlow
   Amidst the moonlight pale,
Two friends kept step beside me,
   Two honest lads and hale.

Now Dick lies long in the churchyard,
   And Ned lies long in jail,
And I come home to Ludlow
   Amidst the moonlight pale.

LIX

THE ISLE OF PORTLAND

THE star-filled seas are smooth to-night
From France to England strown!
Black towers above the Portland light
The felon-quarried stone.

On yonder island, not to rise,
Never to stir forth free,
Far from his folk a dead lad lies
That once was friends with me.

Lie you easy, dream you light,
And sleep you fast for aye;
And luckier may you find the night
Than ever you found the day.

LX

Now hollow fires burn out to black,
  And lights are guttering low:
Square your shoulders, lift your pack,
  And leave your friends and go.

Oh never fear, man, nought's to dread,
  Look not left nor right:
In all the endless road you tread
  There's nothing but the night.

LXI

HUGHLEY STEEPLE

THE vane on Hughley steeple
  Veers bright, a far-known sign,
And there lie Hughley people,
  And there lie friends of mine.
Tall in their midst the tower
  Divides the shade and sun,
And the clock strikes the hour
  And tells the time to none.

To south the headstones cluster,
  The sunny mounds lie thick;
The dead are more in muster
  At Hughley than the quick.
North, for a soon-told number,
  Chill graves the sexton delves,
And steeple-shadowed slumber
  The slayers of themselves.

To north, to south, lie parted,
  With Hughley tower above,
The kind, the single-hearted,
  The lads I used to love.
And, south or north, 'tis only
  A choice of friends one knows,
And I shall ne'er be lonely
  Asleep with these or those.

LXII

"TERENCE, this is stupid stuff:
You eat your victuals fast enough;
There can't be much amiss, 'tis clear,
To see the rate you drink your beer.
But oh, good Lord, the verse you make,
It gives a chap the belly-ache.
The cow, the old cow, she is dead;
It sleeps well, the horned head:
We poor lads, 'tis our turn now
To hear such tunes as killed the cow.
Pretty friendship 'tis to rhyme
Your friends to death before their time
Moping melancholy mad:
Come, pipe a tune to dance to, lad."

Why, if 'tis dancing you would be,
There's brisker pipes than poetry.
Say, for what were hop-yards meant,
Or why was Burton built on Trent?
Oh many a peer of England brews
Livelier liquor than the Muse,
And malt does more than Milton can
To justify God's ways to man.
Ale, man, ale's the stuff to drink
For fellows whom it hurts to think:
Look into the pewter pot
To see the world as the world's not.
And faith, 'tis pleasant till 'tis past:
The mischief is that 'twill not last.

Oh I have been to Ludlow fair
And left my necktie God knows where,
And carried half-way home, or near,
Pints and quarts of Ludlow beer:
Then the world seemed none so bad,
And I myself a sterling lad;
And down in lovely muck I've lain,
Happy till I woke again.
Then I saw the morning sky:
Heigho, the tale was all a lie;
The world, it was the old world yet,
I was I, my things were wet,
And nothing now remained to do
But begin the game anew.

Therefore, since the world has still,
Much good, but much less good than ill,
And the sun and moon endure
Luck's a chance, but trouble's sure,
I'd face it as a wise man would,
And train for ill and not for good.
'Tis true, the stuff I bring for sale
Is not so brisk a brew as ale:
Out of a stem that scored the hand
I wrung it in a weary land.
But take it: if the smack is sour,
The better for the embittered hour;
It should do good to heart and head
When your soul is in my soul's stead;
And I will friend you, if I may,
In the dark and cloudy day.

There was a king reigned in the East:
There, when kings will sit to feast,
They get their fill before they think
With poisoned meat and poisoned drink.
He gathered all that springs to birth
From the many-venomed earth;
First a little, thence to more,
He sampled all her killing store;
And easy, smiling, seasoned sound,
Sate the king when healths went round.
They put arsenic in his meat
And stared aghast to watch him eat;
They poured strychnine in his cup
And shook to see him drink it up:
They shook, they stared as white's their shirt:
Them it was their poison hurt.
—I tell the tale that I heard told.
Mithridates, he died old.

LXIII

I hoed and trenched and weeded,
  And took the flowers to fair:
I brought them home unheeded;
  The hue was not the wear.

So up and down I sow them
  For lads like me to find,
When I shall lie below them,
  A dead man out of mind.

Some seed the birds devour,
  And some the season mars,
But here and there will flower
  The solitary stars,

And fields will yearly bear them
  As light-leaved spring comes on,
And luckless lads will wear them
  When I am dead and gone.